there is no power on earth that can neutralize the influence of a high pure simple and useful life

RFB 1999

Distilled Wisdom for Growing Older Without Growing Old

by Pamela Harman Daugavietis

Those who tell the stories rule society.
—Plato (429 to 347 B.C.E.)

There's no such thing as an uninteresting life, such a thing is an impossibility. Beneath the dullest exterior, there is a drama, a comedy, a tragedy.
— Mark Twain (1835-1910)

How wonderful it is that nobody need wait a single moment before starting to improve the world.
—Anne Frank (1929-1945)

Balboa Press books may be ordered through booksellers or by contacting:

Balboa Press
A Division of Hay House
1663 Liberty Drive
Bloomington, IN 47403
www.balboapress.com
844-682-1282

ISBN: 979-8-7652-5308-3 (sc)
ISBN: 979-8-7652-5307-6 (e)

Library of Congress Control Number: 2024911638

Print information available on the last page.

Balboa Press rev. date: 07/15/2024

BALBOA.PRESS
A DIVISION OF HAY HOUSE

COVER: Reb Robert's 3ft. x 2 ft. 9-inch painting has graced my home office every day since 1999 when I bought it from Reb[1] himself. This colorful image of Uncle Sam[2] paired with Booker T. Washington's[3] potent quote caught my eye 25 years ago and inspires me even more today. The reason? On July 4, 2026, we Americans will be celebrating the 250th anniversary of our founding. According to the World Economic Forum, the United States of America is the only country in the world to reach such a milestone.

And why is this? Ever since its founding, the United States of America has been a symbol of freedom for people around the world who know freedom isn't free. Meaningful work gives our lives purpose and meaning. Diversity is a strength not a weakness. Every life matters. We all have the potential to achieve whatever we were born to achieve. Regardless of creed, color, gender, age, spiritual beliefs and faith traditions, as well as other life circumstances, we Americans are free to enjoy the benefits of being ourselves. Each one of us is unique from every other person who ever lived, with our own story and our own experiences. By doing so, we affirm Aristotle's wisdom: the whole is greater than the sum of its parts.

We who are older have gained not only knowledge and experience, but also wisdom, which Booker T. Washington's quote assures us. Our beloved U.S. can and *will* continue to grow stronger as we who are growing older physically are growing stronger in spirit. By passing on our hard-earned wisdom, hopefully we can and will inspire our own younger citizens, and older and younger citizens in other countries around the world, to do the same.

If only one story in the pages that follow inspires you to begin writing your own stories for your personal joy and pleasure today and for those coming after you, I will feel grateful, knowing my time spent writing and publishing this book was well worth the effort.

---

[1] Reb Roberts is a popular Folk Artist in Grand Rapids, Michigan: www.sanctuaryfolkart.com/gallery

[2] The origin of the term Uncle Sam, though disputed, is usually associated with a businessman from Troy, New York, Samuel Wilson, known affectionately as "Uncle Sam" Wilson.

[3] Booker Taliaferro Washington was an American educator, author, orator, and adviser to several presidents of the United States..

Contents

Introduction

I am a part of all that I have met; yet all experience is an arch
wherethro' gleams that untravelled world whose
Margin fades for ever and ever when I move.

—From *Ulysses* by Tennyson

~

If there are two things I've learned in eight decades of living, it's that everyone has a story—unique yet similar to everyone else—and that no one, no matter their age or life circumstances, is irrelevant.

I was reminded of this once again last fall when our server at Bob Evans Restaurant in Worthington, Ohio, asked my husband Andy and me, my sister Marcia and brother-in-law Marvin where we were from. I told him Andy and I were in town for my 80th birthday celebration last evening with 30 of my classmates who graduated together from Worthington High School in 1961.

"Wow, that's impressive," he said. "Why, all 30 of you are like walking libraries." Honestly, I had never thought of myself as a walking library, or anyone else for that matter. Reflecting on this wise, middle-aged man's insightful metaphor of a life well-lived as we drove back home to Michigan, I thought about how he was a walking library, too. Each year of life is like a book, each day like turning a page. We share our common humanity yet each one of us is unique, different from every other human being who ever lived. We learn from the past by honoring the past for wisdom gained and lessons learned. Yet we live, learn, and love in the present to positively affect our daily and future lives, as well as the lives of others.

Writing these stories and publishing this book has been a journey back in time for me—a journey of gratitude rather than wistfulness and regret. Admittedly, growing older has not been what I would call a piece of cake, both physically and psychologically. Truth be told, I never thought I'd be this old, and sometimes I do long for the 'good old days'!

As our dear friend Bill Martindill, who died at age 100, always said, "Growing older is inevitable; growing old is optional." My desire not to be stuck in the past continues to be as strong as my desire to live with joy, gratitude, purpose and meaning every day of my life going forward as long as I can. Hopefully, a few of the stories that follow about books I have read and still own will inspire you to write your own stories about things you love, for your enjoyment now and for those coming after you.

Pamela Harman Daugavietis

It is time to browse through the precious books that have meant
the most to you that you may rediscover illuminating
Phrases and sentences to light your pathway to the future...
– Wilferd A. Peterson

Two hardcover books I've owned for more than 30 years also sparked my motivation to begin compiling this collection of distilled wisdom from books, quotes and stories I've written about firsthand experiences.

The first is *Pioneer Women: Voices from the Kansas Frontier* by Joanna L. Stratton, published in 1981. The second is *Distilled Wisdom: An Encyclopedia of Wisdom in Condensed Form*, compiled, edited and published by Alfred Armand Montapert in 1964. Both books are available on Amazon.

Joanna Stratton began compiling *Pioneer Women* in 1975 when she discovered in her grandmother's attic a set of priceless autobiographical manuscripts written by hundreds of women who helped settle the Kansas frontier. Their work was the work of survival and demanded as much from them as from their men. Whether fashioning clothes out of raw wool or homes out of sod, coaxing vegetables out of the sun-parched earth, or defending their cabins against a raid of wolves, these women became equal partners with their husbands.

In the book's introduction, written by Arthur M. Schlesinger, Jr., he writes: "As my father dryly observed sixty years ago in *New Viewpoints in American History*, 'All of our great historians have been men and were likely therefore to be influenced by a *sex* interpretation of history all the more potent because unconscious.' In recent times the women's liberation movement has begun to raise the consciousness even of male historians. The result is the belated recognition that women have been around, too, and that life could not have gone on without them."

Interesting to note that in 2025, *Pioneer Women* will have been published 45 years ago, and Arthur M. Schlesinger, Jr. refers to his father who wrote *New Viewpoints in American History* 60 years before that in 1920. I've been seeing the word 'herstory' in use more often today which I gladly welcome. Makes me wonder if an updated title for Schlesinger's father's book could be titled *New Viewpoints in American History and Herstory*, a term that came into use in the 1960s, meaning written from a feminist perspective emphasizing the role of women told from a woman's point of view.

I bought my copy of *Pioneer Women* the year it was published after listening to it on Radio Reader over our local PBS radio station shortly after I was divorced and still living in Petoskey. My copy of *Distilled Wisdom: An Encyclopedia of Wisdom in Condensed Form*, 344 pages of quotes—mostly by men—was a gift from my Aunt Charlotte's 80-year-old mother-in-law Ruth Harvey who felt sorry for me as a newly divorced, single mother in a man's world. There are no stories or explanations about why or when the quote was written, where it originally appeared or under what circumstances. I never read it cover to cover, and rarely have Montapert's quotes been useful or inspiring to me except for one: *"There has been a woman at the beginning of all great things,"* attributed to Alphonse Lamartine, a French author, poet, and statesman.

Certainly women were *equal partners* with their husbands on the American frontier in the 1880s, so hearing their stories over the radio and then reading the same stories in a book published years after pioneer women wrote in their own words about their sacrifices, hardships and simple joys they experienced more than 100 years ago, gave me the courage to not give up when I faced what felt like insurmountable odds in the 1980's.

Fast forward to the end of the 20th century with several quotes from Christine Mary McGinley's powerful and seminal book, *The Words of a Woman*, published in 1999:

"It would be a thousand pities if women wrote like men, or lived like men, or looked like men, for two sexes are *quite* inadequate, considering the vastness and variety of the world, however would we manage with only one? *Male* and *female* are in fact perpetually passing into one another. There is no wholly masculine man, no purely feminine woman. The true feminine is beyond the whole question of subjection and domination and inequality. It is the catalytic power which is essential to all creativity. As long as humanity continues to evolve, to separate ourselves from the chaos, to express ourselves in a higher form, we must create. With the active involvement in restoring the true feminine energy there lies great hope. We could all be among those who, with Rodin, *bow* before the toilsome effort of the thinker, and who, with Pasteur, 'never doubt that knowledge and peace will triumph over ignorance and war.'"

Books, Stories and Quotes

*If and when the grid goes down, I always have
a book to read, a candle to light and extra
batteries for my flashlight.*
—Pamela Harman Daugavietis

*You pay a heavy price when you get all your
information from only one source.*
—Dr. Andrew Daugavietis

*My goal in sharing the wisdom I've gained
through experience—both good and bad—
is to give you hope in **your** life.*
—Richard M. DeVos[4]

Downsizing the more than 500 books I've saved over the years has taken me more time and energy than I first imagined. Once I realized I couldn't keep all of them, I chose 25 books by various authors—in the order in which I read them—to have close at hand as long as I live.

In the stories that follow, all written in 500 words or less, I've attempted to describe what I learned from each book that either challenged, or inspired me when I first read it, and why its wisdom continues to sustain me as I grow older. I love how Jack Kornfield defines wisdom as "seeing things as they *really* are," which you'll read more about on page 35.

As you read (or only leaf through) these stories, imagine each one as a one-of-a-kind hors d'oeuvre (French for appetizer). Sample or taste each one, some you may love, others not

---

4   Co-founder of Amway, founded in 1959 in Ada, Township, Michigan, from DeVos's book *Hope From My Heart: Ten Lessons for Life*, published in 2000.

so much. Remember, these are from my point-of-view, from my firsthand experiences. Your point-of-view may be entirely different from mine, but we learn from each other when we share our stories—and grow wiser, too. As my older sister Barbara always said, "You don't have to make someone else wrong to make yourself right."

Next, reflect on your own decades of living, learning and loving. What activities growing up or later in life have given you the most joy and pleasure: hiking, biking, painting, volunteering, collecting antiques, shoes, baseball cards, or rocks—the possibilities are endless. My hope is that you, dear reader, will be inspired to write stories about your own firsthand experiences and why your memories of them still matter to you.

What joy, pleasure and well-earned wisdom from decades of living have they given or affirmed for you to pass on to those coming after you? Tips on how to get started begin on page 58.

*It is better to trust in the LORD than
to put confidence in man.*

–*The Holy Bible*, King James Version, Psalms 118:8

In 1951, Grandmother Harman, my father's mother, gave me my King James Version of the Bible for Christmas, signing it, "For Pamela Sue Harman from Grandmother Harman, December 25, 1951. Be sure to read it and learn how to use it much and well."

Other than looking up certain verses from time to time, I never read Grandmother's Bible cover to cover after she gave it to me. What I do remember in the spring of 1979, the night I realized my marriage was over, I took Grandmother's Bible to bed with me. Holding it close to my heart, I prayed and prayed until I fell asleep that somehow God would guide me through the days, weeks and months ahead. I knew I couldn't get through alone whatever was to come for my sons John and Bob, their father, and me. Although I felt my life was over, I didn't want to do anything to cause more pain, especially for my sons.

Some 10 years later when Andy and I went to Saudi Arabia, I took Grandmother's Bible with me, risky but worth it since Bibles and Christian jewelry with crosses, were forbidden. After returning from Saudi Arabia, it took me years to realize I could never have gone to Saudi Arabia and leaving my sons John, 20, and Bob, 17, behind if it hadn't been for their stepmother they loved and who loved them. Choosing to go with Andy and without my sons was the most difficult, yet one of the best decisions I ever made.

After Andy and I settled into our new home in Grand Rapids, Michigan, in 1991, I met my good and longtime friend Jane who told me about a verse in Grandmother's Bible that affirmed all the difficult decisions I had ever made: Psalm 118:8, "It is better to trust in the LORD than to put confidence in man." What amazes me is that this verse is in the exact middle of the Bible between the shortest chapter of the Bible (Psalm 117) and the longest (Psalm 119), on page 563. Also, there are 594 chapters before Psalm 118, and 594 chapters after it–594 x 2 equals 1,188. Happenstance or intentional on God's part?

Since realizing most of the books on the following pages were written by men, I sometimes wonder if the Bible was written entirely by men, too. Perhaps we'll never know. I've always regarded the Old Testament as 'an eye-for-an-eye-and-a-tooth-for-a-tooth' stories while the New Testament tells stories about why Jesus came to Earth, not to start a new religion, but to help Jewish people and people of faith traditions from around the world live together in peace. To me, Jesus' greatest teaching is found in Matthew 22; 37-39: "Thou shalt love the Lord thy God with all thy heart, and with all thy soul, and with all thy mind. And the second is like unto it, Thou shalt love thy neighbor as thyself."

Wilbur never forgot Charlotte. She was in a class by herself. It is not often that someone comes along who is a true friend and a good writer. Charlotte was both.

—*Charlotte's Web*, by E.B. White, ©1952

I first read *Charlotte's Web* by E.B. White in 1952, the year it was first published. I was nine and loved it so much I read it twice. Since then, I've periodically revisited many parts of it. I also fondly remember reading my original copy aloud to my two sons, when they were growing up. What I loved most about E.B. White's classic, enhanced by black and white drawings by Garth Williams, was how E.B. White wrote about life, and death, friendship and change, how time passes quickly, never to go backwards, only forward.

I could relate to Fern's response on page one when her mother told her the baby pig was a runt and "will never amount to anything."

"Do *away* with it," shrieked Fern." You mean *kill* it? Just because it's smaller than the others?"

Perhaps this was because when my two sisters and I were growing up, we had a dad who had a heart for small and vulnerable animals. We had a baby skunk he rescued that we named Sammy, two baby chicks that became large ducks named Mack and Quack, and two canaries named Pete and Skeet.

What I consider to be the essence of *Charlotte's Web* is the unlikely friendship between a pig and a spider, a pig saved by a little girl's compassion and a spider's uncanny ability to spell words in her web that saved her friend's life. And then when Charlotte's life was coming to an end, she created her egg sac, her best work, a "peach-colored cocoon that looked as though it were made of cotton candy" she called her *magnum opus*. "Your future is assured," she told Wilbur. "You will live secure and safe. Nothing can harm you now." And Wilbur, overcome with emotion responded, "Oh, Charlotte, to think that when I first met you I thought you were cruel and bloodthirsty. Why did you do all this for me? I don't deserve it. I've never done anything for you." Charlotte replies, "You have been my friend, in itself a tremendous thing. I wove my web for you because I liked you. After all, what's a life anyway? We're born, we live a little while, we die."

Charlotte's best work after saving Wilbur's life was her children, the baby spiders who would hatch with all but three of them flying away. Joy, Aranea and Nellie were there to stay in Wilbur's pen until the end of his life.

Every life has purpose and meaning, every life has worth, just as Charlotte's and Wilbur's did, including the legacy they left behind.

Pamela Harman Daugavietis

*It's really a wonder that I haven't dropped all my ideals, because
they seem so absurd and impossible to carry out.
Yet, I keep them, because in spite of everything I still
believe that people are really good at heart.*

–*The Diary of a Young Girl* by Anne Frank, ©1993

I read *The Diary of Anne Frank* for the first time when I was 13. Reading about her life in hiding from July of 1942 to August of 1944, made me question why I had such a good life when other girls my age in other parts of the world didn't. Even though Anne was older than me, I felt a special kinship with her. She was born on June 12; I was born on May 12. She loved many of the same things I loved—reading, writing, and spending time with friends.

Reading Anne's diary, published in 1952 by Anne's father, Otto Frank, opened my eyes and heart to a much larger world I wanted to better understand so I could hopefully do something when I became an adult to help correct the imbalances that caused so much suffering for so many. Although I no longer have my original copy I read in 1953, I've purchased and still own subsequent editions of Anne's diary, including the one above. Anne died of malnutrition and typhus at Bergen-Belsen, in either late February or early March of 1945, six months before U.S. President Truman announced the end of World War II.

To me, Anne Frank's is the most notable and enduring voice to come out of WWII, the deadliest military conflict in history. An estimated 70–85 million people perished. Yet Anne took her suffering and turned it into a strength of spirit, a deeper appreciation for what truly matters in life by writing stories that continue to inspire millions of others including me. She realized every life has significance as a gift of inestimable worth, and accepted that no life is without suffering and loss. Anne knew intuitively the power of stories to heal, to enlighten, to inspire and to touch the hearts of readers to positively change the world for the better in their own lives, through their own stories. According to the Anne Frank Center (www.annefrank.com), Anne's diary has been translated into 70 languages with over 30 million copies sold. Today, Anne's story is especially meaningful to young people because of increasing political and religious unrest throughout our world. For many she is their first, if not their only exposure to the history of the Holocaust. Hopefully, future generations of leaders in all nations will come together to find ways for a peaceful and prosperous way forward for everyone regardless of race, religion, gender, ethnicity and politics.

Pamela Harman Daugavietis

For oft when on my couch I lie,
In vacant or in pensive mood,
They flash upon that inward eye,
Which is the bliss of solitude;
And then my heart with pleasure fills,
And dances with the daffodils.

by William Wordsworth (1770-1850)

–One Hundred and One Famous Poems,
Roy J. Cook, Editor, ©1958

Daffodils have always held special meaning for me. The large bed of bright, yellow daffodils burst into full bloom every spring in our backyard in the 1950's on Clearview Avenue in Worthington, Ohio. Mother, who loved to garden, planted them herself. Among other flowers she planted on all sides of our large, corner lot, daffodils were the first to appear. Unlike most tulips and other spring flowers, daffodils are truly perennial, resilient even when temperatures drop in the ever changing spring weather.

Mother belonged to a group of longtime friends, housewives and homemakers like Mother who called themselves "The Daffodils," although I'm not sure why. Perhaps it's because they saw themselves as beautiful, dependable and resilient. When I was in high school, I belonged to Girls' Ensemble, and one of my favorite *a cappella* songs we sang was William Wordsworth's *The Daffodils*.

Sometime between my senior year in high school and my sophomore year in college, I bought a paperback copy of *One Hundred and One Famous Poems* because it contained Wordsworth's poem about daffodils. Sadly, I later misplaced or lost my original copy of the book having moved 14 times from the time I left home in 1966 until Andy and I settled in Grand Rapids, Michigan, in 1991, a span of 25 years.

Imagine my surprise and delight when my dear son and daughter-in-law, John and Amy, gifted me a leather-bound copy of my beloved pocket-sized book of poetry for my 52nd birthday, nearly 30 years ago. When I need to step away from whatever's going on, I take my book of poems down off the shelf, sit, read, recover and regroup.

The Daffodils isn't the only poem in my keepsake book of poetry I always want close at hand for inspiration and comfort. Others include *The Rhodora* by Ralph Waldo Emerson, *Trees* by Sergeant Joyce Kilmer, *Ode on Intimations of Immortality* by William Wordsworth, *Thanatopsis* by William Cullen Bryant, *Invictus* by William Ernest Henley, *If* by Rudyard Kipling, *Nobility* by Alice Cary, and many others.

As Editor Roy J. Clark writes in the preface: "*This is the age of science, of steel—of speed and the cement road. The age of hard faces and hard highways. Science and steel demand the medium of prose. Speed requires only the look—the gesture. What need then for poetry? Great need! There are souls in these noise-tired times, that turn aside into unfrequented lanes, where the deep woods have harbored the fragrances of many a blossoming season. Here the light, filtering through perfect forms, arranges itself in lovely patterns for those who perceive beauty.*"

Pamela Harman Daugavietis

Mankind is made of star stuff, ruled by universal laws. The
thread of cosmic evolution runs through his history,
as through all phases of the universe . . .
Evolution is still proceeding in galaxies and man,
to what end we can only surmise.

—The View from a Distant Star: Man's Future In The Universe
by Harlow Shapley, ©1963

I n the fall of 1963, during my sophomore year at Ohio State, my grades began to slip from A's to C's after my boyfriend I thought would be my husband someday broke up with me. I decided to switch from Arts and Sciences to the School of Journalism after my mother soothed my wounded ego and told me I was a communicator and born to be a writer. The following summer, I applied for a job as an editorial clerk at the *Columbus Citizen-Journal*, our morning newspaper, five days a week from 4 to 11 p.m. I could still attend classes at Ohio State during the day and take the bus from campus to downtown. My parents would pick me up at 11 every night. My first day was September 8, 1964.

My job entailed delivering mail on three floors and making regular coffee runs for editorial staff and reporters to a restaurant down the street, gathering obituaries for print from various sources, and gathering news clips from the Associated Press and United Press International ticker-tape machines. Every so often, City Editor Bill Moore (no relation as my mother's maiden name was Moore) told the three of us clerks to pick out a newly published book from a dozen or so he'd lay out on the conference table, read it, and write a brief review for Friday's newspaper. One book that caught my eye and is still in my personal library is *View from a Distant Star: Man's Future in the Universe* by Harlow Shapley, published in 1963 by Dell Publishing, Inc. Its opening paragraph (see above) stunned me then and stuns me still today.

Shapley's opening paragraph continues here, and is why I am concerned about our collective future: *Is humanity here to stay? Can humans survive the rigors of their harsh environment?*

They themselves have made it harsh by adding to the natural hazards greater ones of their own making. Population pressures and the fruits of their science and technology now threaten their future. Our lifetime on our small planet will depend on how well humans understand the requirements for survival and how willing they are to struggle for the peaceful creation of a viable world society. (Full disclosure, I edited the word 'men' to 'humans' and pronouns accordingly, as well.)

My view after eight decades of living, learning and reading books is that once the imbalance between male and female energies come into better parity, we humans will achieve higher collective consciousness. Working together with heads and hearts, we will find sustainable solutions to the many complex problems and conflicts we face together today. Once we humans are able and willing to come together in our diversity and evolve from an 'either/or' to a both/and view, we will not only survive but also thrive. The legacy we leave behind will assure that generations coming after us will continue to thrive as well.

Everything can be taken from a man but one thing:
the last of the human freedoms—to choose one's attitude
in any given set of circumstances, to choose one's own way.

–*Man's Search for Meaning* by Viktor Frankl, ©2006

Somewhere between my sophomore and senior years at Ohio State, I read *Man's Search for Meaning* for the first time. Having been born in 1943, in the middle of WWII, I always had a personal interest in why we have wars and what we can do today to avoid WWIII. Perhaps Frankl's classic written in 1959, one of 39 books, some written before he became a prisoner of war, should be required reading today for all Americans old enough to read. In his last paragraph of *Man's Search for Meaning* he closes with, ". . . man is that being who invented the gas chambers of Auschwitz; however, he is also that being who endured the gas chambers upright, with the Lord's prayer and the Shelma Israel on his lips."

My original copy, published in 1962, was eventually lost, so I bought the updated copy above that includes a postscript by Frankl, written in 1984, which concludes with: "So let us be alert—alert in a two-fold sense: Since Auschwitz we know what man is capable of. And since Hiroshima we know what is at stake."

As I re-read the underlined parts of Frankl's timeless book, and there are many, I realize they are as pertinent now as they were when they were written. In addition to the one at the top of this page, two of my other favorites are: "When we are no longer able to change a situation, we are challenged to change ourselves;" and, "Those who have a 'why' to live, can bear almost all 'how'." Frankl's 'how' in Auschwitz and later Bergen-Belsen was his love for his wife of only nine months, Tilly, who later died in Bergen-Belsen.

Frankl's explanation of the power of love is a message to us to truly appreciate what we have today, now, in our family and friend relationships and with the one we share our life with. He says that love is the only way to truly appreciate someone in the innermost core of their being. He said love gives us the ability to see the essential and best traits and features of our beloved which may not be actualized yet, but eventually will be actualized by the power of love itself.

I will close with a distillation of another timeless quote by Frankl in *Man's Search for Meaning* that speaks to the importance of those of us who are growing older. "Today's society is characterized by achievement orientation, and consequently it adores people who are successful and happy, especially the young . . . yet it virtually ignores the value of all those who are otherwise, and in so doing, blurs the decisive difference between being valuable in the sense of dignity and being valuable in the sense of usefulness."

*Adopting a middle-of-the-road position is usually just tepidity
and timidity, but to grasp a paradox and to hold it in
tension requires courage and wisdom.*

—The Authentic Person: Dealing with Dilemma
by Sydney J. Harris, © 1972

The Authentic Person: Dealing With Dilemma, is a book I return to often for clarity about the meaning of paradox. As Niels Bohr (1885-1962) the Danish physicist, said, "The opposite of a correct statement is a false statement. But the opposite of a profound truth may well be another profound truth."

I bought the 142-page, pocket-size book in 1972, the year it was published. Its author, Sydney J. Harris, was a favorite daily columnist of mine in the *Detroit Free Press.*

In the book's preface, Harris condenses a series of lectures he gave beginning in the early 1950's. His book attempts to "stimulate thought *about the way we think* with less emphasis on the subjects we think about and more on the process and the person doing the thinking." In other words, he says the person thinking is as important as what they're thinking about.

On page 22, Harris claims our modern dilemmas are mainly caused by either/or rather than both/and thinking, speaking and acting. Examples: right/wrong, male/female, rich/poor, black/white, Republican/Democrat, and so on.

This little booklet helped me become more comfortable with how I describe myself today, in the middle all the way as a middle child, born Methodist, later becoming Presbyterian, and then Catholic when I married Andy. What I sadly discovered, however, were the dualities within Christian churches that all felt they were doing things right and other denominations were doing things wrong—in how they interpreted the Bible and how they practiced their religion.

Which brings up another dilemma I had growing up when preachers I listened to preached about how wonderful heaven was, how eternal happiness awaited us once we died.

And at someone's death, whether expected or unexpected, everyone cried. Our faith tells us only the living grieve; those who die do not, for they are in a better place.

Distilling all the wisdom Mr. Harris shares quite clearly and candidly in this book is impossible. For comfort, I re-read it from time to time when I feel caught between the "right" and "wrong" side of anything, including growing older. Perhaps this is why I became so interested in the life of Buddha who taught "the middle way" as the best way to live, like the Goldilocks Principle, neither too hot nor too cold, "just right," another story for another time.

Indeed, the truth that many people never understand, until it is too late,
is that the more you try to avoid suffering, the more you suffer, because
smaller and more insignificant things begin to torture you, in proportion
to your fear of being hurt.

—*The Seven Story Mountain* by Thomas Merton, ©1976

While preparing to leave for Riyadh, Saudi Arabia 35 years ago as a new bride, the only book I packed was the Bible my Grandmother Harman gave me when I was eight. When Andy and I left Riyadh 19 months later, on January 10, 1991, in addition to my Bible, I packed two more books to bring home with me. The first was *The Seven Story Mountain* by Thomas Merton I bought in our compound's bookstore. The second one was *The Road from Coorain* by Jill Ker Conway. I read Merton's book while in Riyadh and read Conway's book cover to cover on our 26-hour journey home. My friend Rosemary gave me Conway's inspiring book the day she and I said good-bye for the last time before Andy and I left Riyadh for good.

Merton's book, written when he was 31, a recent convert to Catholicism living in a Trappist monastery, didn't make sense to me the first I read it. What I did glean from it then, as a recent convert to Catholicism myself, was how we humans create more suffering for ourselves and others by trying to avoid pain with temporary distractions rather than trying to understand what's causing our pain in the first place. At some point, we must face our suffering, seek help to understand what's causing it and why, and change our ways so we can forgive ourselves as well as others and move on.

Years later I understood the meaning of the title of Merton's autobiography's since he doesn't mention *Dante's Divine Comedy* anywhere in his memoir, *The Seven Story Mountain*. While I never read Dante's 712-page volume written 700 years ago, one of the greatest works in Western literature, I did recently read *A Beginner's Guide to Dante's Divine Comedy* by Jason M. Baxter, a 200-page distilled version of Dante's book. My understanding of it affirms my faith that we perfectly imperfect humans are forgiven by God of all our 'sins', meaning separation from God, when we realize what we did was wrong, correct our ways and forgive ourselves and others. Our mother always told my sisters and me, "Don't judge others until you've walked a mile in their shoes."

Although I doubt if I'll ever read Merton's classic from cover to cover again, it will always be on my bookshelf along with the Bible I received from my Grandmother Harman, and *The Road from Coorain*, from my friend Rosemary. Both are reminders of the power of faith, family, friends and community to overcome all obstacles keeping us from a life of purpose and meaning, prosperity and peace, joy and love.

*Then, when looking back at your life, you will see that
the moments which seemed to be great failures
were incidents that shaped the life you have now.
You realize that nothing can happen
to you that is not positive.*

—*A Joseph Campbell Companion: Reflections on the Art of Living,*
Selected and Edited by Diane K. Osbon, ©1991

Although I had never heard of Joseph Campbell, it was the sub-title at the top of the cover that grabbed my attention. Picking it up and turning it over, I read two timely quotes I needed to hear:

"The privilege of a lifetime is being who you are."

"The goal of the hero trip . . . is to find those levels in the psyche that finally open to the mystery of your Self being Buddha consciousness or the Christ. That's the journey."

All this happened in a bookstore in Chicago in June of 1991. Andy and I were with my two sisters and our brothers-in-law for the weekend. It was our first in-person get-together since he and I returned from Riyadh, Saudi Arabia, to Grand Rapids, Michigan. Marcia and Marvin lived in Worthington, Ohio, where my sisters and I grew up, and Barbara and Jim lived in Winnetka, a suburb of Chicago. Although I was 48, having moved a number of times for various reasons, I occasionally found myself feeling like Dorothy in *The Wizard of Oz,* trying to find my way home, wherever home was.

Yet here Andy and I were reconnecting with my two sisters and our two brothers-in-law, after a long hiatus. Although we girls had occasional disagreements growing up, and dissimilar lifestyles now that we were married with children, we loved each other and were committed to understanding each other better so we could deepen our relationships.

As I started reading *Reflections on the Art of Living,* I felt a kinship with Joseph Campbell, especially on page 62 where he writes, "It takes courage to do what you want. Other people have a lot of plans for you. Nobody wants you to do what you want to do. They want you to go on their trip, but you can do what you want. I did. I went into the woods and read for five years."

While I never wanted to go into the woods for five years, I love to read and write stories. With the help of books and firsthand experience, I can say I've never regretted any choice I ever made. Some were painful, both before and after, yet they all brought me to where I am today, living a perfectly imperfect life with Andy. Together we are learning, loving, laughing and grateful to be here, able to read, write stories, and enjoy family, friends and others we also love, learn from and greatly admire.

Sameness is not oneness. Unity is not uniformity.

—*The Seven Habits of Highly Effective People*
by Stephen Covey, ©2020

Every morning at breakfast, Andy and I take turns reading from four books and two monthly magazines we've collected over the years. Andy reads from three books; I read from one book and two monthly publications.

I sometimes wonder if we only had time to read two books, which ones would we choose? Andy's favorite is *Daily Reflections for Highly Effective People*, a paperback, pocket-size book by Stephen R. Covey (1932-2012). For more than 50 years, I've been subscribing to *Daily Word*, an inspirational monthly magazine (dailyword.com) for all faith traditions. While I am never without my *Daily Word*, even when away from home, I've grown very fond of Stephen Covey's book of daily reflections. Its wide range of subjects and distilled wisdom stay with me throughout my day. I had never read Covey's 440-page book about the seven habits and was curious to learn more, so I bought a copy last year.

Early on, I found *Habit 1: Be Proactive* too detailed, so I started leafing through the first few pages of the other habits. When I came to *Habit 6: Synergies* on page 308, I found this: "*When properly understood, synergy is the highest activity in all life—the true test and manifestation of all the other habits put together.*"

Two more paragraphs down, I found this: "*What is synergy? Simply defined, it means that the whole is greater than the sum of its parts. It means the relationship that the parts have to each other is a part in and of itself. It is not only a part, but the most catalytic, the most empowering, the most unifying, and the most exciting part.*"

Cynthia Bourgeault, a faculty member at the Center for Action and Contemplation (cac. org), describes the foundational principles of the Law of Three as affirming, denying, and reconciling. She says the interweaving of the three produces a fourth in a new dimension. For example, you and I are collaborating on a project. You have an idea about how to get started; I have another idea. While our ideas differ, we can discuss, discern and agree on the best of each idea to create a third idea that's better than either yours or mine.

Full disclosure, I did not finish reading the entire Habit 6 chapter. However, I went back to Habit 1, and will make my way through the book in bits and pieces. I don't want to rush reading this book and then put it back on the shelf feeling proud of myself for having read it. I want to learn from it in increments so I can hopefully live Stephen Covey's *7 Habits of a Highly Effective Life* myself, and at my age, I believe it's better to at least try living them than never to try at all.

Unless I know and understand the family system from which
I came, I will have difficulty understanding
my true self and the society I live in.

—*Bradshaw On: The Family* by John Bradshaw, ©1996

The first edition of *Bradshaw On: The Family* was written in 1988, the result of his popular PBS TV series of the same name. Although I never watched any series segments, I knew it was widely acclaimed so I bought and read his second edition.

What was and remains so appealing to me about Bradshaw's book is his humility, authenticity, and passion for helping individuals and families heal past psychological wounds. Bradshaw shares the whys of his own family's disfunction and how he learned to transform his pain into lessons gained through love. The wisdom he teaches about the importance of healthy family relationships is timeless. Our country needs more of this wisdom today.

In 1996, when Bradshaw's revised edition came out, I was 53, a new Catholic after being a lifelong Christian Protestant, married for seven years to my second husband, with two grown sons of my own, both married, and a grown son and daughter by marriage. To call our family back then complicated, was an understatement. Originally, I called it our "blended" family, but when I realized we were not going to be all alike, I started calling it our "integrated" family. We all learned to get along well because we respected each other's boundaries, something else Bradshaw writes about so well.

As a middle daughter growing up in "the Age of Conformity," I tried to be like everyone else. And then the 60s came, and all the virtues and values I was taught growing up suddenly went passé. Finding my true self wasn't something I had ever thought much about, that is until I graduated from college, married the first time, and realized the Cinderella story with a happily-ever-after ending was an unconscious desire to be taken care of instead of being my own best friend, as my mother always told me to be.

Fast forward to Bradshaw's Epilogue, *Revising Traditional Values*, where he discusses among other things the importance of faith, family, friends and a strong marriage. He also includes forgiveness of self and others since we're all learning as we go. As long as we're alive, we live our lives forward, never backward.

So, thanks to John Bradshaw, who died in 2016 at age 82, the legacy he leaves behind in his book will always be on our bookshelf. Thanks to John Bradshaw and our other many teachers, Andy and I will soon celebrate our 35th wedding anniversary. We are grateful to still be learning, forgiving and loving ourselves while learning from, forgiving and loving each other, just as we learn from, forgive and love family members past, present and future, and new and longtime friends!

*The greatest lesson I have learned is that the universal
must be wedded to the personal to be
fulfilled in our spiritual life.*

—*A Path With Heart: A Guide Through the Perils and Promises
of Spiritual Life* by Jack Kornfield, ©1993

Jack Kornfield's book about the teachings of Buddhism came out the year my mother died shortly after undergoing surgery for a deteriorating heart condition. Mother's death came at a time of major transition for me, as well. Here I was, soon to be 50, and dying to my old self while trying to birth a new self. With Mother's death, another chapter of my life ended, and a new chapter began.

As a lifelong Christian, reading *A Path with Heart* made me think of my mother, whose own life was filled with twists and turns. As a lifelong Christian herself, she lived her values and taught me the importance of being my own best friend. She also often told me, "A lady knows when it's time to leave," whether she meant from a wild party, or at the end of life. Mother certainly walked her talk.

Kornfield describes the spiritual life as being open to change, the everyday impermanence of life. He writes, "Letting go is a central theme in spiritual practice, as we see the preciousness and brevity of life. When letting go is called for, if we have not learned to do so, we suffer greatly, and when we get to the end of our life, we may have what is called a crash course. Sooner or later, we have to learn to let go and allow the changing mystery of life to move through us without our fearing it—without holding or grasping."

So here I am now, beginning the ninth decade of my life, realizing from the time we are born to the time we die we all experience both joy and happiness, suffering and loss. Kornfield says spiritual practice will not save us from suffering and loss. Rather, he says, it allows us to understand that avoidance of pain doesn't help. From a Buddhist perspective, he's saying by honoring our true situation we will find a way through it.

Kornfield's distilled 'take home' for me is the importance of wisdom and compassion—wisdom is seeing things as they *really* are, and compassion is knowing we are all One. As a Christian who tries daily to be a follower of Jesus, my faith in God keeps me going forward when things don't go as I want, knowing God, Christ and the Holy Spirit are with me, supporting me and teaching me every step of the way.

Pamela Harman Daugavietis

By talking or writing about previously inhibited
experiences, individuals translate the event into language.
Once it is language-based, people can better understand
the experience and ultimately put it behind them.

—*Opening Up: The Healing Power of Expressing Emotions*
by James W. Pennebaker, PhD, ©1997

All of us want and need to be noticed and appreciated for what we do and who we are. How many of us know how others see us? We all have a story, and those of us in our older years grew up in a time when children were to be seen and not heard. After modern talk shows such as Oprah and Dr. Phil became popular in the early 2000's, it seemed to me people started talking too much. So where's a middle way to heal hurtful emotions? As my wise and dear friend Diane Zarafonetis taught, "What you can't express you can't heal."

Introducing Jamie Pennebaker, as he prefers to be called, trained as a social psychologist who later became interested in expressive writing. Jamie discovered if people were asked to write about upsetting experiences, doing so improved their mental and physical health. The author of 12 books, Pennebaker has also written more than 300 articles on the power of expressing feelings and emotions through writing. As he says, there's no right or wrong way to do this, and you don't even have to share what you write with anyone but yourself. It's basically learning how to be your own best friend. (Thank you, Mother!)

What's been astounding to me is when I chose the 25 books I wanted to write stories about, I didn't purposely place Pennebaker's book smack dab in the middle. Yet that's where it landed, 13th in a list of 25 books. It's like reading and re-reading the first 12 books helped me climb a mountain, and the last 12 helped me heal so I could be who I truly am and was meant to be.

When I bought *Opening Up*, I not only wanted to help heal my own past traumas, but also to help patients of all ages I interviewed at Butterworth Hospital and Helen DeVos Children's

Hospital for publication in the hospital's Foundation newsletter. Many of them shared with me after their stories were published how healing it was to see their stories in print that were read and acknowledged by others who felt healed by them, too.

After reading Pennebaker's book, I learned how to ask questions that would help them come up with answers to better process their experience of being hospitalized. Many of them were able to return to school or work and continue with their lives. Others, who were not expected to live, not only survived but thrived because of the compassionate lifesaving care they received. I often think of the many patients I interviewed, wondering where and how they are today, trusting they were able to fulfill the dreams they described to me and live lives of purpose and meaning.

Creation is as ongoing as we are; as vast as our
experience of it. It is in us and we in it;
it is us and far beyond us.

–Original Blessing by Matthew Fox, ©2000

When Andy and I returned from Saudi Arabia in 1991 and settled in Grand Rapids, Michigan, I was more than grateful to be home. But my adjustment as a new Catholic, a stepmother to a son and daughter with a mother of their own while my two sons had a step-mother they loved and who loved them, was a challenge for me. Getting through those initial first years and the years since was only made possible by my faith in God and Andy by my side.

Somehow, I heard about Matthew Fox and began listening to his tape about the four paths of a spiritual journey: the Path of Awe (via positiva), the Path of Release (via negativa), the Path of Creativity (via creativa), and the Path of Transformation (via transformativa). I was especially enlightened to hear for the first time Meister Eckhart's teachings about how we're not born sinners, we're born to create, to say "yes" to life. Ever since I first either heard it or read it, I have loved Eckhart's famous quote, "If the only prayer you ever pray is thank-you, it will be sufficient."

Meister Eckhart (1260-1328) teaches that God loved us first so we can love ourselves first and love others better. He reminds us in his writings that we sin, meaning we separate ourselves from our Creator God, but we are not essentially sinners. To me, this means that nobody is born evil; babies' lives are shaped by how they are welcomed into the world, how they are loved and taught right from wrong, how they are guided to become who God created them to be, endowed with gifts only they can give to a world in need of their unique contributions.

Eckhart teaches that Jesus came to Earth to show us that being human is good, and we are forgiven when we realize what we did was wrong. Being human is a gift from God. We are born, we live and learn to love self and others, and when we die, we return to God as spiritual beings having a human experience, as taught by Pierre Teilhard de Chardin. When we die as humans, we return to our Source as spirit. Matter is created out of the energy of love that changes form but cannot be destroyed, for love is timeless, eternal, everlasting. Such knowledge helped me become more accepting of difficult experiences as lessons to be learned rather than something to be feared, including growing older and accepting my own passing from this life when the time comes.

The metamorphosis from Old Testament into Gospel
is not an exclusively intellectual development;
it is the crisis itself that matures.

–Things Hidden Since the Foundation of the World
by René Girard, ©1987

After I heard about the teachings of philosophical anthropologist René Girard, I bought his book in 2016, hoping it would help me better understand why we humans keep waging wars against each other. In other words, what are the root causes of the Old Testament 'eye for an eye' way of settling disagreements?

While much of Girard's book was beyond my ability to understand, what I have gleaned from it is what I feel is his greatest wisdom—we humans create our own reality by choices we ourselves make in our own thoughts, words and actions.

Things Hidden Since the Foundation of the World contains a comprehensive overview of Girard's work as a reflection on the Judeo-Christian teachings. The book is a dialogue between Girard and psychiatrists Jean-Michel Oughourlian and Guy Lefort about Girard's three core human characteristics. These behaviors influence our social interactions with others without us being aware of them, due to our need to evolve to a higher consciousness:

Mimesis: the process by which individuals copy one another in escalation, leading to conflict because of desire for looks, wealth, fame and power. In other words, Girard's idea proposes that all desire is merely an imitation of another's desire, and the desire only occurs because others have said the object desired is worthwhile.

Scapegoating: a process by which collective guilt is transferred onto victims, and because they've been eliminated so has our guilt, or so we thought. The scapegoat mechanism has one requirement for it to be effective in restoring peace; all those who helped in the removal of the scapegoat must genuinely believe that he is guilty. Because it's essential to keep the scapegoat from striking back, he is killed.

Violence: using physical force to injure and harm animals, or property, with pain, death, damage and/or destruction; getting 'even' rather than communicating, cooperating and collaborating to find peaceful solutions to disagreements and disorder. Girard teaches that humans imitate each other which gives rise to rivalries and violent conflicts. Such conflicts are partially solved by scapegoating—killing the one deemed responsible for the conflict, which is why Jesus was killed. But by His example, Jesus taught us not to hate our enemies, rather to love and forgive them instead. As Christians, we are called to do the same, but how many of us are doing this today?

Ultimately, Girard, who says Christianity is the best antidote to violence, himself became a committed and practicing Roman Catholic after reading *The Brothers Karamazov* by Fyodor Dostoyevsky—another book for another time.

One reason so many people have lost heart today
is that we feel both confused and powerless.

—*The Wisdom Pattern: Order, Disorder, Reorder*
by Richard Rohr, ©2020

Although she was seven years younger than me, my friend Colby, who died of cancer five years ago, was one of my teachers. Colby was Catholic and the first person to tell me about Father Richard Rohr, a Franciscan priest at the Center for Action and Contemplation in Albuquerque, NM. Fr. Rohr and I were both born in 1943, although he was born a Catholic in Kansas, and I was born a Methodist in Ohio.

What was so enlightening and inspiring to me were Fr. Rohr's daily emails, as they still are today. Messages he writes himself or those written by others are the first I read every morning, like a pep pill for the mind and heart. I still own more than 30 of Fr. Rohr's books. One that stands out is *The Wisdom Pattern: Order, Disorder, Reorder.*

In it, Fr. Rohr remains faithful to the Catholic Church while writing about ways the church must change in order to attract new and younger members. He isn't saying to let go of the teachings of the past but shares ways of applying them in today's changing world. Life growing up was different for those of us born in the mid-1900s, than it was for our grandparents and parents. Life changed for our children when they were growing up in the late 1990s. And how quickly it's changing today for those born since the beginning of the third millennium.

Paragraph one of Chapter One begins with Fr. Rohr saying: "One reason so many people have lost heart today is that we feel both confused and powerless. Paragraph two of Chapter One begins with, "This became even more evident after the horrific terrorist attacks of September 11, 2001. Everything that had seemed so important—stock options, consumer choices, increasingly affluent lifestyles—suddenly faded. Church attendance increased immediately."

Anyone born say after 2007, likely has no memory of 9/11. While many are aware of this pivotal event, living through something so devastating to our nation and to the world is vastly different than reading about it in a book. This doesn't diminish the value of books and reading, but to me, this underlines the importance of writing about our first-hand experiences, both facts and feelings. Generations coming after us can and will better understand the emotional impact history has on those who live through it.

And while Colby and I can no longer meet for lunch and talk about all kinds of things both silly and serious, spending time with her will always be among my fondest memories, and always grateful she told me about Father Richard Rohr when she did.

*To become whole is to become harmoniously fully
functional. In such a reality, you treat yourself
and others with unconditional love and care.*

The Shift: The Revolution in Human Consciousness
by Owen Waters, ©2006

In the November 2001 issue of the Institute of Noetic Sciences newsletter, Christopher Bache calls 9/11 a "crisis in consciousness." I'm not sure I understood the full meaning of the word 'consciousness' before seeing that in print, describing the horrific, life-changing event that happened two months earlier. How could we, the leaders of the free world—so intelligent, so evolved, so powerful— have made ourselves so vulnerable to Middle Easterners traveling to America on one-way tickets, without luggage and with the goal of destroying our country?

How did 19 men—15 from Saudi Arabia, two from United Arab Emirates, one from Lebanon and one from Egypt—manage to hijack four commercial airliners with the intent to destroy the World Trade Center's twin towers, the Pentagon and White House or Capitol, taking more than 3,000 innocent lives with them? Both the White House and Capitol were spared because of the heroism of Todd Beamer, 32, and 39 men and women on United Flight 93, who chose to do the right thing at the right time. Their actions required the greatest sacrifice. Beamer's last recorded words were, "Are you guys ready? Let's roll."

Five years after 9/11, I bought Owen Waters' newly published, 160-page book, *The Shift: The Revolution in Human Consciousness*, understood about half of it, and was inspired to hopefully someday understand the rest of it.

What I love is how Waters encourages us and supports us in learning how to live our lives as "cultural creatives," first described by Paul Ray and Sherry Anderson in their book, *The Cultural Creatives*, published one year before 9/11. Ray and Anderson describe Cultural Creatives as those who "love nature, respect the Earth and are deeply concerned about the environment. They like to develop close relationships with each other, and to help and encourage other people to develop their abilities. They care about personal and spiritual development and want more equality for women and all cultural groups."

Waters says psychologist Abraham Maslow (1908-70) became famous for identifying our basic needs as humans—food, shelter, safety and security, acceptance by others and becoming part of a group, a tribe, an extended family or community—before we can evolve to a higher consciousness, which Waters calls 'The Shift'. Many today are urging *all* ages to, "change your thinking, change your life," and "thoughts become things." So, dear friends, it's never too late. As long as we're breathing, we're still learning, and slowly but surely shifting into a higher consciousness.

Pamela Harman Daugavietis

We are not human beings having a spiritual experience.
We are spiritual beings having a human experience.

—Teilhard's Mysticism: Seeing the Inner Face of Evolution
by Kathleen Duffy, SSJ, ©2014

W hen I first read that Jesuit Priest Pierre Teilhard de Chardin was the source of the above quote, I wanted to learn more about him. Although it's still being debated whether or not he was the source of this quote, his teachings align with what this quote affirms for me. My faith has always assured me that we humans come from God to Earth as spirit and return to God as spirit when we die.

Teilhard, a Jesuit priest with a PhD in paleontology from the Institut Catholique de Paris, was part of the team that discovered the 350,000-year-old Peking man. Born in Auvergne, France, Teilhard's writings were banned by the Catholic Church for bringing science and religion together, a both/and approach to living our faith. In 1951, he moved to New York City where he died in 1955 at age 74.

To me, Teilhard is a true follower of Christ because he did not resent those who rejected him or exclude those some considered deplorable. He endured suffering without giving up, maligning his critics and compromising the truth of his faith. Doing so, he left a legacy that continues to inspire me and millions of others around the world.

Shortly after I learned about Teilhard, Andy and I spent time in Aix-en-Provence. We were surprised to learn that in 1899 at age 18, Teilhard entered the Jesuit novitiate in Aix-en-Provence. Curious to know more about the school Teilhard attended, we spoke to the librarian there who seemed knowledgeable about Teilhard's teachings, but said he wasn't well known among the French themselves, which surprised us.

After we returned home, Andy and I became lifetime members of the American Teilhard Association (teilharddechardin.org). I purchased Dr. Kathleen Duffy's book *Teilhard's Mysticism* which helped me better understand Teilhard's teachings. In 2019, I purchased her newly published book, *Teilhard's Struggle: Embracing the Work of Evolution*. I learned the Church suppressed Teilhard's writings because they were gaining such wider appeal and seemed in conflict with the Church's stand on Modernism.

After Teilhard's death, Pope John Paul II, Pope Benedict XVI, and Pope Francis all made positive comments about Teilhard's writings that continue to gain wider appeal around the world.

When Andy and I learned Teilhard is buried in Hyde Park, New York, we visited there not once but twice to pay honor and respect to a man who continues to teach us and so many others about who we are, where we've come from and why we're here, which is all about love, *Lasting, Omnipresent, Vital, Energy.*

Fostering our creativity in older age benefits us by
strengthening our morale later in life,
contributes to improved physical health as
we age, enriches our relationships
and is our greatest legacy.

—*The Second Half of Life: Opening the Eight Gates of Wisdom*
by Angeles Arrien, ©2007

For all her academic credentials and accomplishments, Angeles Arrien was one of the most authentic, humble, kind, wise and evolved persons I ever had the honor of meeting and speaking with one-on-one. I met her in July of 1996 at the Institute of Noetic Sciences annual conference, and bought the book she is most famous for, *The Four-Fold Way: Walking the Paths of the Warrior, Teacher, Healer and Visionary* published in 1993.

In beautiful handwriting, she signed, "For Pam, With respect to you and your gifts, Angeles." I wish I had written to her to tell her how much her encouraging words meant to me back in my early 50s when my self-confidence was at an all-time low, and how her written words mean a lot to me yet today as I enter my early 80s. Unfortunately, Angeles died of pneumonia in 2014, yet her legacy lives on as her books are growing in popularity.

Over a period of 24 years, Angeles Arrien published nine other major works bridging anthropology, psychology, and religion, all translated into many different languages. I also bought her book *The Signs of Life: The Five Universal Shapes and How to Use Them*, winner of the 1993 Independent Book Publishers Benjamin Franklin Award. *The Signs of Life* has a preferential-shapes test I took several months ago that, if anything, has validated my writing of *Distilled Wisdom*, which I see as my way of sharing what I've learned and am learning while acknowledging those who have taught me so much through their lives and writings.

The third book I bought by Angeles is *The Second Half of Life,* published in 2005 and winner of the 2007 Nautilus Book Award for Best Book on Aging. Thus, this is the book I chose to highlight of her three books I will always have in my personal library.

In her introduction, Angeles begins with, "There are more of us entering the second half of our lives than at any other time in history. Our numbers are growing rapidly, and as life expectancy continues to rise, more of us will find ourselves living much longer as elders than did our parents and grandparents."

She goes on to say, these extra years, even decades, extend the blessings of life. Yet in many ways we are not prepared to live these years fully. Our American culture has lost the capacity to acknowledge, and value elders the way many other cultures around the world do." And I say, "Amen, amen," with the hope that this changes soon.

*It's a thrill to fulfill your own childhood dreams,
but as you get older, you may find that enabling
the dreams of others is even more fun.*

–*The Last Lecture* by Randy Pausch, ©2008

Although Dr. Randy Pausch (pronounced powsh) was only 47 when he died, he was as wise as any human being I've ever known about. When asked to give a lecture about the disease that would soon take his life, he accepted the challenge, even though he only had months to live. Hesitating at first, on Sept. 18, 2007, he told his audience he intended to have fun until his end came and advised others to do the same. Dr. Randy Pausch, professor of Computer Science, Human-Computer Interaction, and Design at Carnegie Mellon University in Pittsburgh, Pennsylvania, died 10 months later.

Diagnosed with pancreatic cancer in August 2006, Dr. Pausch, a husband and father of three young children, had choices to make about how he would spend the last few months of his life. Little did he know at the time that he would soon become famous for sharing his journey with the world.

Dr. Pausch delivered his last lecture, titled *Really Achieving Your Childhood Dreams*, to a packed auditorium at Carnegie Mellon University. The lecture was recorded on video for those unable to attend. By December, the video made its way to YouTube. More than 7 million views later, Dr. Pausch was known worldwide. His simple, uncomplicated messages appealed to viewers of all ages and backgrounds. Shortly afterward, he and Jeffrey Zaslow, a columnist for the *Wall Street Journal*, teamed up to write *The Last Lecture*, an international bestseller that's been translated into 30 languages.

After giving his lecture and co-writing his book, Dr. Pausch could have retreated quietly to his home to spend time with family and friends. Instead, he made an extraordinary choice and decided to use the time he had left to speak on behalf pancreatic cancer patients worldwide. He felt a remarkable sense of responsibility that gave his life new purpose and meaning, something we all need, especially as we grow older. Dr. Pausch also knew that our written stories and wisdom will help those coming after us create their own evolutionary lives. In March of 2008, just days before he was scheduled to testify before Congress, Dr. Pausch was hospitalized for three days with renal failure and congestive heart failure, all side effects of his ongoing treatment.

In his last lecture and through his advocacy efforts, Randy Pausch left gifts of hope and optimism for patients and loved ones touched by pancreatic cancer. I would add that he also left behind gifts of hope to millions of others, including me. His book has inspired me to have the courage when the time comes to emulate how he faced the end of his life by telling those he was leaving behind that despite everyday challenges everyone faces sooner or later, including impending death, to have fun every day, too.

Suffice it here to say that abandonment in any of its myriad forms is the greatest and most damaging fear a human infant-child can undergo.

—The Heart-Mind Matrix: How the Heart
Can Teach the Mind New Ways to Think
by Joseph Chilton Pearce, ©2012

Nearly 30 years ago, Joseph Chilton Pearce was scheduled to present a program I had signed up for at an Institute of Noetic Sciences conference in California. At the last minute, he was unable to attend, a huge disappointment to me. Even so, I came to the conference and purchased five of his books. I read all five and still own four of them.

Lately, I've been thinking about Joe, as he preferred to be called, especially as college graduations here in America continue to be disrupted by students and non-students demonstrating for Palestinians and against Israelis. The first question I would ask him is, "What are the root causes for this violent disruption of year-end classes and graduations for college students across our country? Why are so many violating the rights of those who have spent fours years and paid large sums of money to become educated, and are now unable to celebrate their accomplishments together and with their families?

Of the four, *The Heart-Mind Matrix* encapsulates what I feel are Pearce's greatest teachings on human and child development, a distillation of his other books. My interest in how children develop into stable and effective adults is a result of having had parents who loved me and being a mother myself, plus my career as a free-lance writer for Butterworth Hospital in the early 90s, and later for Helen DeVos Children's Hospital. What I learned from NICU doctors and nurses, child psychologists and educators, children and their parents, is that the first three years of a child's life are foundational.

In his writings, Pearce describes the difference between human minds and human hearts and how they work together or apart by choices we ourselves make and the consequences of both. The head or mind energy he calls 'intellect', is more about ego and male energy. Intellect, he says, asks, "Can I/we do it?" The heart energy he calls 'intelligence', is more about compassion and female energy. Intelligence, he says, asks, "Should I/we do it?" Pearce says we need both head and heart working together, a both/and approach to living, learning and loving. All of us, regardless of our gender at birth, have both male and female energies, some more of one than the other. It's how we choose to use these energies, whether consciously or unconsciously, that creates our day-to-day reality.

One of Joe's most insightful quotes: "Our razor-sharp intellect can create and build atom bombs and destroy the very atmosphere of our Earth, but the basic intelligence needed to grasp the fundamental problem of loss of nurturing *is gained only by brain-heart development itself.*"

Faith is in the spirit; faith knows that God has
given us everything now, and that it is His will
that all our prayers should be answered now.

The oldest book I own is a 98-page, hardcover, pocket-sized book titled *The Hidden Truth* by Christian D. Larson. Published in 1907, the year my mother was born, the book first belonged to my father's father. On the inside cover of his book, Grandfather signed "E. H. Harman," in perfect penmanship. When he died, the book was handed down to my Aunt Hannah, who later passed it on to her son, my cousin, John Harman "Jack" Dickey. In 2018, several years before Jack died of multiple sclerosis at age 79, he passed the book to me.

Grandfather also underlined passages that also have special meaning to me. If, however, I were asked to edit and update them for the 21st century, I gladly would, not in substance, but in the choice of words.

For example, on the title page is printed in capital letters: THERE IS SOMETHING IN MAN THAT MAKES ALL THINGS POSSIBLE. I would change this to lowercase and change 'man' to 'every individual'.

On page 3, the first two sentences read: "To him who has faith all things are possible. Faith is that something in man that transcends every form of limitation and opens the mind to the limitless powers of the soul." My version would replace 'him' with 'those,' and 'man' with 'all individuals'.

On page 10, Grandfather noted the following phrase in pencil, none of which I would change: "Whatever we may desire to accomplish, nothing is more important than to be able to draw upon the limitless for thought, ideas, plans, methods, wisdom, power, inspiration, in brief, everything that one may require to take advantage of every opportunity."

Even though this book was written over 100 years ago, its message is pertinent yet today, and perhaps even more so given our highly complex and complicated world. As the last lines in this little book I've edited affirm, "Faith is the hidden secret to every human desire and need; therefore, all things are possible to those who have faith; and all things desired shall come to those who live, think and act in the very soul of that faith that is faith."

A paperback edition of *The Hidden Truth* is available today on Amazon for $6.49.

Pamela Harman Daugavietis

*Even when we go astray, God continues to love us
unconditionally and sends his Son to bring us back home.*

An Explorer's Guide to Julian of Norwich
by Veronica Mary Rolf, ©2018

What endeared Julian of Norwich to me the first time I heard about her is that she refers to our Creator as Father/Mother God—shocking to her contemporaries and still shocking to some today. As a woman whose real name is unknown and who survived the Black Plague in 13th century England, Julian also became the first female to write a book in English.

Today, many books are available about Julian by various authors, including Veronica Rolf, Mirabai Starr and Mathew Fox and the 16 visions she had of Christ and the Virgin Mary she calls 'showings.' While I have read and still own books by all three authors, I chose Rolf's book to focus on because of how she organizes its content. In Part I, "Getting to Know Julian of Norwich," she asks, "Why Julian Now? In Part II, she provides a guided tour of Julian's *Revelations of Divine Love.*" She explains the phrase Julian is well known for, "all shall be well, all manner of things shall be well."

For me, what's so remarkable about Julian is that she lived during a time when women and children were silenced. Julian was only six when the first wave of the Great Pestilence arrived in Europe, killing millions of people, including, it is thought, a third of her immediate family. As a female, Julian was not allowed to go to school beyond puberty. By the time the second cycle of the plague returned—in 1361—Julian was 19 and may have been married with a young child, like most women of her time. Philosopher and theologian Grace M. Jantzen wrote that Julian was possibly a widow whose husband and children perished in what she calls the Black Death, as Julian's tender writings about the importance of motherhood were based on her own firsthand experience.

In Julian's book, *Showings*, she writes: "This fair and lovely word, mother, is so sweet and so kind in itself that it cannot truly be said of anyone or to anyone except of him and to him who is the true Mother of life and of all things. To the property of motherhood belongs nature, love, wisdom and knowledge, and this is God."

Every year, thousands of tourists make a pilgrimage to Julian's reconstructed anchorage in Norwich, England, to sit and pray where Julian herself sat and prayed. Rolf adds, "Perhaps they also come to wonder: What would make a woman choose to be permanently enclosed in a one-room cloister for some 25 years in order to devote her life to prayer, contemplation, and the writing of her *Revelations?*"

Julian's writings and life, despite her unbelievable sufferings, have inspired and continue to inspire me as I grow older in a world that feels chaotic yet capable of overcoming chaos with love.

Simplicity means to feel such a strong sense of
kinship with others that, as Gandhi said, we 'choose
to live simply so that others may simply live.'

—Choosing Earth: Humanity's Journey of Initiation Through Breakdown
and Collapse to Mature Planetary Community,
by Duane Elgin, ©2022

In the early 1990s, I attended a lecture at the Fetzer Institute in Kalamazoo, Michigan, presented by Duane Elgin. During his talk, Elgin predicted that by 2020 to 2025, masses of immigrants would enter by foot into Europe from Syria and other Middle Eastern war-torn and destabilizing countries, and into the U.S. from Mexico and South America for the same reasons. Impressed by his prescience and obvious concern about the future of our country and world, I went up afterward to personally thank him.

As we all know, Elgin's predictions have come true. More immigrants are entering the U.S. illegally from Africa and China, as well as from other unstable countries around the world, and/or those experiencing food shortages and autocratic regimes.

Like me, Elgin was born in 1943, so he's now in his ninth decade of life and reminding all of us that since the beginning of time, wars have not ended conflict. In a "winner-vs.-losers world," wars have caused both sides to press the 'pause button' for a time, that is until "the other side" decides to rearm and fight back.

On his personal website duaneelgin.com, Elgin is informing us once again what we must do to avert more war and what some call Armageddon and the Apocalypse:

1. **Choosing Earth**: Humanity is in an unprecedented whole systems crisis. What path do we choose?

2. **Citizen Voice initiatives:** How an Earth-Voice movement can awaken and empower citizens of the Earth.

3. **Voluntary Simplicity**: Compassionate ways of living that are outwardly simple, inwardly rich, and serve the wellbeing of all life.

4. **The Living Universe:** Rich insights about the universe as a living system transform our sense of identity and evolutionary journey.

On his other website, choosingearth.org, Elgin shares numerous resources describing the challenges and opportunities for anyone desiring to play a positive role in our great transition as a global community.

In *Choosing Earth*, Elgin defines compassionate simplicity as "a feeling, a strong sense of kinship with others that, as Gandhi said, we 'choose to live simply so that others may simply live.' Compassionate simplicity means feeling a bond with the community of life and being drawn toward a path of reconciliation—especially with other species and future generations. Compassionate simplicity follows a path of cooperation and fairness, seeking a future of mutually assured development for all."

I would rather do penance all at once; let me die.
I cannot endure captivity any longer.

Joan of Arc by Mark Twain, ©1989

I can't recall what it was about the last book Mark Twain ever wrote that first caught my attention. Yet after reading it and telling my husband about it, Andy read Twain's 452-page book *Joan of Arc*, too. We both loved it.

Originally published in 1895 and 1899, it took Twain 10 years to research and write. He considered it the best book he had ever written, dedicating it to his wife, Olivia, on their 25th wedding anniversary. The story of their somewhat unusual meeting and love affair is beautifully captured in another book about Twain I also recently read, *Mark Twain: A Life*, Ron Power's 720-page book published in 2005.

Born Samuel Langhorne Clemens in 1835, in Florida, Missouri, to John and Jane Clemens, Sam grew up with three brothers and a sister named Pamela. Their father died when Sam was 12, so the family had to make their own way in the world as best they could.

When he turned 28, Sam became a newspaperman in Nevada and adopted the pen name Mark Twain, referring to his steam-boating days on the Mississippi River. The measure of the depth of the water was expressed with a crewman's cry "mark twain!," meaning two fathoms, or 12 feet.

It is said that Mark Twain's lifelong compulsion was to capture life with words. During the years leading up to, during and after the Civil War, he used humor to better understand the human condition and to get his audience to laugh together to create a better way forward for America. He loved traveling and exploring new countries, and he and Olivia, 'Livy' for short, traveled around the world in spite of Livy's failing health as they grew older. Although well-traveled, Mark Twain was a true blue American, which may be part of the reason he admired Joan of Arc so much. She gave her life for a cause she believed in and in doing so, inspired the French to fight for their freedom, too.

In no way can I distill the entire contents of *Joan of Arc* in this brief review of why both Andy and I found this book such a treasure. Thus, I will quote from page 422 in Powers' book, *Joan of Arc*, where he describes Joan as "an icon of the century and a repository for its tortuously shifting view of womankind: a virginal innocent devoted to the hearthside and the spinning wheel, she was also a leading figurehead for women in the military as she took command of her nation's armies at age 17, led them to the lifting of the English siege of Orleans, which hastened the end of the Hundred Years War and the liberation of France. Later, she was burned at the stake as a heretic, a fate that perhaps served to temper the male anxiety about her menace as a role model."

Timeless Treasures

Shortly after my mother's death in 1993, I compiled the following list of childhood messages from our mother—Mary Ellen Harman—as we were growing up. I've always called them "Stick With ME Messages," since most of them came from her. Truth-be-told, several came from both our parents. Without a doubt, they have stood the test of time and have helped me get through ups and downs all my life. As we who are now in our 'older years' know, our world today is changing faster than when we were growing up, and it seems to be speeding up every day.

Thus, as I continue downsizing my files, books, clothes, household and personal odds and ends and various writings I've done in the past, I don't want to "throw the baby out with the bathwater." These messages are still helpful to me today, and have value and relevance for me as I live the last decades or years of my life. As Robert Frost's poem, "Stopping by Woods on a Snowy Evening" says:

> *The woods are lovely, dark and deep,*
> *But I have promises to keep,*
> *And miles to go before I sleep,*
> *And miles to go before I sleep.*

Instead of complaining about growing older, I'm vowing to strive to make the years ahead among the best years of my life in spite of physical and emotional challenges. As long as we're breathing, we are alive and learning and loving not only what was, but what is to come in the next great adventure.

Stick With ME Messages

Learn to make do or do without.

People watch too much television.

Don't believe everything you read in the newspaper.

Don't go looking for trouble.

Be trustworthy.

Know how to keep a secret.

Just because everyone's doing it doesn't make it right.

Keep your eyes and ears open and your mouth shut.

There's always a wrinkle under the rug somewhere.

A place for everything and everything in its place.

If you take care of everything you have you'll never be poor.

Waste not, want not.

Actions speak louder than words.

Don't judge others until you've walked a mile in their shoes.

Be your own best friend.

Pamela Harman Daugavietis

"Learn to make do, or do without."
—Mary Ellen Moore Harman

Making Do

Back in the first decades of the 20th century, when my mother and her family lived on a small farm in rural Newark, Ohio, her father sold buggy whips for a living. My mother's mother, my grandmother, took care of their four young children and kept up a household without telephone, electricity or running water. My grandparents didn't have enough money to buy ice cream, so they made their own in the winter with fresh fallen snow. Grandma sprinkled it with sugar and added a few drops of vanilla and they all loved it.

Mother told us this story when my sisters and I were growing up, so of course, we wanted to try making snow ice cream, too, but not because we couldn't buy real ice cream at the store. We made it after a new winter snowfall because it was something fun, creative and different to do. "Making do" meant "putting on our thinking caps" when we didn't have something we wanted, or enough money to buy it.

I also recall when Mother drove sister Marcia up to the Home Market in Worthington where we grew up shortly after Marcia and Marvin were married. Mother waited in the car while Marcia went in to pick up a pound of ground round she had ordered for a recipe she was making for friends she and Marvin had invited for dinner that night. Marcia came back to the car to tell Mother she didn't have enough money to pay for the ground round. (This was before credit cards.) Rather than give Marcia the money which Mother could easily have done, Mother thought for a moment and said, "I have a delicious recipe for a main course that calls for plain hamburger."

Marcia went back in, bought a pound of hamburger, and Marcia and Marvin's dinner party was a huge success.

Life Lessons from The School of Life

by Andy and Pam Daugavietis

Don't get all your information from one source.

Begin with the end in mind.

Spend less than you earn and invest the difference.

Do little things well and you'll do big things better.

There's no age limit on learning.

Don't make someone else wrong just to make yourself right.

Be yourself, everyone else is taken.

Do what you love and love what you do for a purposeful life.

Make a living by what you earn; make a life by what you give back to help others.

Growing older is inevitable; growing old is optional.

We live our lives forward and understand them backwards.

Synergy joins the best of both sides for a win/win outcome.

Learn from the past, live in the present to shape a better future.

If you can dream it, you can do it.

To whom much is given, much is expected in return.

Epilogue

My vision for America is a united, integrated, both/and country, not politically, culturally and racially divided.

When we go back to our roots and core virtues and values our forefathers and foremothers lived by to settle this land from the beginning, we'll be reminded that personally and collectively, freedom is hard work.

All of us, regardless of our age or life circumstances, are capable of doing what we can and must in our daily lives to assure that America will always be a welcoming home to those who value freedom, justice and peace. We honor and learn from the past, but we live in the present as we shape our personal and collective future.

On June 19, 1885, the Statue of Liberty, inscribed with the words below from *The New Colossus*, a poem by Emma Lazarus (1849 –1887), was delivered to the shores of America as a gift from the French people. Lady Liberty, as she is also known, was a gift in commemoration of France's alliance with the United States during the American Revolution. Our Statue of Liberty stands as a vision of hope that democracy in America will prevail and that freedom and justice for all will be lastingly attained.

> *Give me your tired, your poor, Your huddled masses yearning to breathe free,*
> *The wretched refuse of your teeming shore.*
> *Send these, the homeless, tempest-tossed to me,*
> *I lift my lamp beside the golden door!*

Appendix

The Pearl of Great Price

Again, the kingdom of heaven is like unto a merchant man, seeking goodly pearls: Who, when he had found one pearl of great price, went and sold all that he had, and bought it.

– Matthew 13:45-46, King James Version

Think of life-story writing, or of writing a letter to leave behind for your children and grandchildren, nieces, nephews or friends, as writing a story about your own "pearl of great price." What do you want them to know about you, or your life, that might be helpful for them as they continue living into a future you can only dream about. No complaining, no negative opinions about the world today, no axes to grind, no grudges to settle. Rather, share with them what you've learned about how to stay strong in your own convictions when facing disappointment, loss, conflicts at work or at home or in your neighborhood, or what you would do differently if you could do it over.

Guidelines to Consider

- One size does not fit all. Do this in a way that's comfortable for you.
- Write a letter in your own handwriting. Or . . .
- Write a story about an event in your life when you learned the most valuable lesson you've never forgotten, something that guides your way even today.
- Stories are more personal, more engaging, and show cause and effect.

Pamela Harman Daugavietis

- If you have more than one event like the *Pearl of Great Price*, write that story, too, and as many stories as you can think of that were life-changing experiences and insights still relevant today.
- Make a list of the 5 or 10 major turning points in your life. Write a story about each one. You don't have to start with the first one. Do them randomly. You can put them in chronological order later.
- Use writing materials you find most comfortable: (1) computer, or (2) pen and paper, or (3) pencil and paper. If you prefer writing by hand, I recommend a spiral notebook with lined, three-ring paper. This way, you can rip out pages to discard later, or place them into a three-ring notebook as you organize your stories according to a timeline or subject matter. To write by hand, I prefer a Pilot refillable pen, fine, 0.7 black ink pen.
- Date each entry.

More Guidelines

A short story can be anywhere from 500 to 5,000 words in length. Advice from E. B. White's *Elements of Style*: "be clear and precise, avoid fancy words, omit needless words."

Other story ideas: list values you strive to live by, values you've had through life. List people who inspired you and why. List hobbies you love, and why.

What you're doing is a natural desire for those in the last stage of life. (Check out Erik Erikson's nine stages of life on the Internet.)

Each one of us can choose whether we see these years as wisdom years while reflecting on our life with gratitude, humility and a sense of humor and staying as active and engaged in life as we can. Or, if we are in despair because of regrets, fear of death, fear of the unknown, we become tempted to give up.

Instead, we make a choice between what Erikson defines as "Wisdom or Ego integrity versus despair"—a choice affecting the "65-and-on" age group. During this time, we have reached the last chapters in our lives. Retirement is approaching or has already taken place and boredom sets in. "What's next?" we wonder.

After the gift of life, the greatest gift Our Creator has given us is the gift of choice: accepting the fact that everyday life brings changes. We can accept these changes and "make lemonade out of lemons," or we can complain and give up. Never!

Ego-integrity means the acceptance of life in its fullness: a both/and approach to life where our victories and defeats, what we accomplished and what we didn't accomplish are part of our story. Wisdom is the result of successfully completing this final developmental task, to die (or pass on to the Next Great Adventure) feeling complete with our lives while leaving behind a legacy of love for those coming after us.

Even More Guidelines for Memoir or Life Story Writing

1. Begin with why, why am I writing this and what do I want to express and share?

2. There is no right, wrong or just one way to write your life story.

3. Honor your ancestors; you're alive because they survived and so can you. Thank those who strengthen you with love and guidance; forgive those for what they did or said that wounded you. Pass on the wisdom you learned without passing on the pain of what they did or said to you. Be your own best friend and let them stay in the past as you go forward in your own life.

4. When you write your life story, don't let anyone else hold the pen.

5. What you can't express you can't heal; write from your head, heart and soul—all three.

6. Reinforce the values you learned, especially those you learned the hard way, for they are like gold.

7. Words have power; choose them carefully. They can and do harm self and others, and they can heal every hurt of the heart.

8. Once in print, always in print; date everything you write when you write it and read it over carefully before it's printed and shared.

9. We change and evolve, what was written yesterday may not be who we are today, and we'll have more to write tomorrow.

10. We live to learn, love, and laugh, and to be able to laugh at ourselves and with others, never at others, is the best medicine of all.

11. Growing older is inevitable; growing old is optional. Old is stuck in the past. Wise is learning from the past, honoring the good of the past while living in the present to positively affect our future and the future of others.

12. When telling the truth in an over-arching narrative it's autobiography; if it's fiction, it's fictionalized truth. Stories are stories that stand alone and stand together as life lived, day by day, hour by hour, minute by precious minute.

KISS: Keep It Simple, Sweetie!⁵

1. **Beginning**: Start with a good beginning that gets your attention quickly.

2. **Lead Character:** Describe at least one character (yourself) you really care about, a character who stays in your heart and mind.

3. **Plot**: Your plot is a series of events that take place, the action of your story that drives your narrative forward.

4. **Action**: Describe a big scene where you take some action to solve the problem.

5. **Ending**: Close with a good ending that keeps your reader wanting to turn the page to the next chapter of your life and pulls your whole life story together.

---

⁵ Ideas taken from a blackboard in the early 1990's in Mr. Waldvogel's 5ᵗʰ and 6ᵗʰ grade English classroom at the Hillsdale Academy, in Hillsdale, MI.

Pamela Harman Daugavietis

Closing Caveats

- Life story writing can be destructive if used to "get even" or cast blame. Be aware of any negative emotions such as unresolved anger, resentment or regret you might be holding around past events or losses. Journaling is an effective way to express emotions in order to heal them. Write by hand from your heart, re-read what you've written, feel the emotion, then consciously decide to release it and shred your writing.

- Forgiveness is a choice we can make today that has the power to free us from a hurt that once expressed and transformed can make us stronger, wiser and more compassionate toward ourselves and others. None of us is perfect and all of us have the power to choose to change our thinking so we can change the direction and quality of each and every day of our lives.

- Taking responsibility for our choices today by choosing to release negative emotions from the past is the beginning of personal freedom, the freedom to be who you were born to be.

- Once you know your story and who you truly are, forgive yourself and others, let go of your story and live life going forward as an authentic, fully alive, awake and aware human being. Our past can be healed in the present and our present thoughts, words and actions affect our future and can affect the future of those we interact with every day. Live consciously in ther present and your life will be a gift to you and everyone whose life you touch, simply by being your true self. Be yourself; everyone else is taken.

Bibliography

Arrien, Angeles, *Signs of Life: The Five Universal Shapes and How to Use Them* ©1992

Arrien, Angeles, *The Second Half of Life* ©2007

Atkinson, Robert, *The Gift of Stories: Practical and Spiritual Applications of Autobiography, Life Stories and Personal Mythmaking* ©1995

Baxter, Jason M., *A Beginner's Guide to Dante's Divine Comedy* ©2018

Bradshaw, John, *Bradshaw On: The Family* ©1996

Brooks, Arthur C., *From Strength to Strength: Finding Success, Happiness and Deep Purpose in the Second Half of Life* ©2022

Brumet, Robert, *Birthing a Greater Reality: A Guide for Conscious Evolution* ©2010

Bucko, Adam, *Let Heartbreak Be Your Guide: Lessons in Engaged Contemplation* ©2022

Butcher, Carmen Acevedo, *Practice of the Presence* ©2022

Chittister, Joan, *The Gift of Years: Growing Older Gracefully* ©2008

Clayton, Eric A., *Cannonball Moments: Telling Your Story, Deepening Your Faith* ©2022

Cobbs, Elizabeth, *Fearless Women: Feminist Patriots from Abigail Adams to Beyoncé* ©2023

Coelho, Paulo, *The Alchemist: 30th Anniversary Edition* ©2018

Conway, Jill Ker, *The Road from Coorain* ©1989

Cook, Roy J., *One Hundred and One Famous Poems* ©1958

Covey, Stephen, *The Seven Habits of Highly Effective People* ©2020

Delio, Ilia, *Birth of a Dancing Star: My Journey from Cradle Catholic to Cyborg Christian* ©2019

Duffy, Kathleen, *Teilhard's Mysticism: Seeing the Inner Face of Evolution* ©2014

Eger, Edith, *The Choice: Embrace the Possible* ©2017

Eger, Edith, *The Gift: 12 Lessons to Save Your Life* ©2020

Elgin, Duane, *Choosing Earth: Humanity's Great Transition to a Mature Planetary Civilization* ©2022

Pamela Harman Daugavietis

Fox, Matthew, *Original Blessing* ©2000

Fox, Matthew, *A Way to God: Thomas Merton's Creation Spirituality Journey* ©2016

Fox, Matthew, *Naming the Unnamable: 89 Wonderful and Useful Names for God . . . Including the Unnamable God* ©2018

Frank, Anne, *The Diary of a Young Girl* ©1952

Frankl, Viktor E, *Man's Search for Meaning* ©2006

Gies, Miep and Gold, Alison Leslie, *Anne Frank Remembered: The Story of the Woman Who Helped to Hide the Frank Family* ©1987

Girard, René, *Things Hidden Since the Foundation of the World* © 1987

Harris, Sydney J., *The Authentic Person: Dealing With Dilemma* ©1972

Hollis, James, *Living Between Worlds: Finding Personal Resilience in Changing Times* ©2020

Jacobs, Harriet, *Incidents of a Slave Girl* © 2020

Johnson, Robert A., *Owning Your Shadow: Understanding the Dark Side of the Psyche* ©1991

Kornfield, Jack, *A Path With Heart: A Guide Through the Perils and Promises of Spiritual Life* ©1993

Larson, Christian D., *The Hidden Secret* ©1907

Lesser, Elizabeth, *The Seeker's Guide: Making Your Life a Spiritual Adventure* ©1999

Levine, Stephen, *Healing Into Life and Death* ©1987

Luke, Helen M., *Old Age: Journey Into Simplicity* ©1987

Lynch, Thomas, *The Undertaking: Life Studies From the Dismal Trade* ©1997

Matousek, Mark, *Writing to Awaken: A Journey of Truth, Transformation & Self-Discovery* ©2017

McKinney, Jane, and McKSchmidt, Mary, *Miracle Within Small Things* ©2023

Merton, Thomas, *The Seven Story Mountain* ©1976

Meyer, Joyce, *How to Age Without Getting Old: The Steps You Can Take Today to Stay Young for the Rest of Your Life* ©2021

Miller, James E., and Cutshall, Susan C., *The Art of Being a Healing Presence: A Guide for Those in Caring Relationships* ©2001

Montgomery, Ben, *Grandma Gatewood's Walk: The Inspiring Story of the Woman Who Saved the Appalachian Trail* ©2014

O'Donohue, John, *Anam Cara: Spiritual Wisdom From the Celtic World* ©1997

O'Murchu, Diarmuid, *In the Beginning was The Spirit: Science, Religion and Indigenous Spirituality* ©2012

O'Murchu, Diarmuid, *Incarnation: A New Evolutionary Threshold* ©2017

Osbon, Diane K., *A Joseph Campbell Companion: Reflections on the Art of Living* ©1991

Palaver, Wolfgang, *René Girard's Mimetic Theory* ©2013

Pausch, Randy, *The Last Lecture* ©2008

Pearce, Joseph Chilton, *The Death of Religion and the Rebirth of Spirit: A Return to the Intelligence of the Heart* ©2007

Pearce, Joseph Chilton, *The Heart-Mind Matrix: How the Heart Can Teach the Mind New Ways to Think* ©2012

Pennebaker, James W., *Opening Up: The Healing Power of Expressing Emotions* ©1997

Pipher, Mary, *Writing to Change the World* ©2006

Pipher, Mary, *Women Rowing North: Navigating Life's Currents and Flourishing as We Age* ©2019

Rohr, Richard, *The Wisdom Pattern: Order, Disorder, Reorder* ©2020

Rohr, Richard, *Everything Belongs: The Gift of Contemplative Prayer* ©2003

Rohr, Richard, *Falling Upward: A Spirituality for the Two Halves of Life* ©2011

Rohr, Richard, *The Enneagram: A Christian Perspective* ©2013

Rohr, Richard, *Everything is Sacred: 40 Practices and Reflections on the Universal Christ* ©2021

Rolf, Veronica Mary, *An Explorer's Guide to Julian of Norwich* ©2018

Savary, Louis M., *Teilhard de Chardin The Divine Milieu Explained: A Spirituality for the 21st Century* ©2007

Shapley, Harlow, *The View From a Distant Star: Man's Future in the Universe* ©1963

Stapanek, Mattie J.T., *Journey Through Heartsongs* ©2001

Singh, Kathleen Dowling, *The Grace in Dying: A Message of Hope, Comfort, and Spiritual Transformation* ©1998

Singh, Kathleen Dowling, *The Grace in Aging: Awaken As You Grow Older* ©2014

Smart, Elizabeth, *My Story* ©2013

Starr, Mirabai, *The Showings of Julian of Norwich: A New Translation* ©2013

Stone, Richard, *The Healing Art of Storytelling: A Sacred Journey of Personal Discovery* ©1996

Strunk, Jr., William, and E.B. White, *The Elements of Style, Fourth Edition, with Revisions, an Introduction, and a Chapter on Writing* ©2000

Taylor, Daniel, *Tell Me A Story: The Life-Shaping Power of Our Stories* ©1996

Teilhard de Chardin, Pierre, *The Phenomenon of Man* ©1959

Teilhard de Chardin, Pierre, *Human Energy* ©1962

Thomas, Cal, *A Watchman in the Night: What I've Seen Over 50 Years Reporting on America* ©2023

Tolle, Eckhart, *The Power of Now: A Guide to Spiritual Enlightenment* ©1999

Van Dyke, Michael, *Radical Integrity: The Story of Dietrich Bonhoeffer* ©2001

Twain, Mark, *Joan of Arc* ©1989

Whyte, David, *Crossing the Unknown Sea: Work as a Pilgrimage of Identity* ©2001

White, E.B., *Charlotte's Web* ©1952

Zweig, Connie, *The Inner Work of Age: Shifting from Role to Soul* ©2021

Thank You

Just as everyone is a walking library, none of us walks through life alone. Writing a book isn't something we do alone either. It takes faith, family, friends, neighbors, colleagues and members of our community to inspire us to create anything, while supporting and encouraging us as we do.

Once I had a rough draft of my book, I sent it to a a few family members and friends who provided enough positive feedback to keep me writing. I also sent a first draft of my story about Pierre Teilhard de Chardin to author Kathleen Duffy who immediately made excellent corrections and suggestions I gratefully incorporated.

Three dear and longtime friends, Marty, Irma and Georgia, offered ongoing support and encouragement that kept me going toward the end when I needed it the most. As it turned out, Irma, for 33 years my newly retired colleague and friend, became my assistant editor, spending hours making a number of suggestions and edits that greatly improved the clarity, accuracy and focus of my book. Thanks to all of you for the roles you played, this book is a reflection of the importance of lasting friendships through 'thick and thin' as we all grow older and wiser together.

Lastly, and most importantly, I want to acknowledge my husband who always encourages me to do what I love, which is to write stories and enjoy life. Together we've shared many experiences here at home and in our travels I never would have experienced alone. Without Andy's loving support, enthusiasm and encouragement for living the life of my dreams, I couldn't and most likely wouldn't have written and published this book.

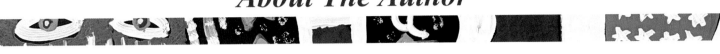

About The Author

Pamela Harman Daugavietis grew up in Worthington, Ohio, the middle daughter of a middle-class family in the middle of WWII and considers herself "in the middle all the way" regarding politics, religion, and life in general, a both/and approach to life rather than either/or. After graduating in 1965 from The Ohio State University School of Journalism in Columbus, Ohio, Pam's life evolved through marriage, motherhood, divorce and starting a mailing and secretarial service in Petoskey, Michigan.

In 1989, she and Andy married and together signed a two-year contract with King Fahad National Guard Hospital in Riyadh, Saudi Arabia, where Andy became a staff rheumatologist and Pam became the first Christian, Western, female writer for the hospital's Public Affairs Department. In 1991, the couple moved to Grand Rapids, Michigan, where Andy joined a local medical practice and Pam became a freelance writer for Butterworth, Spectrum Health and later Helen DeVos Children's Hospital foundations.

In 2008, Pam served as executive producer of *The Gift of All, A Community of Givers*, a one-hour documentary about the history of giving in West Michigan, available today on YouTube. In 1999, Pam self-published *Women's Voices, Women's Visions: A Book of Days for the third Millennium* in memory of Diane Zarafonetis who started the first support group for women with breast cancer in West Michigan. In 2011 Pam wrote *Through the Eyes of a Child: The Story of Helen DeVos Children's Hospital* that tells the story of how and why the hospital was first opened 31 years ago as the first full-service children's hospital in West Michigan.

In 2015, Pam published *Coming Home to Myself: A Memoir* about her experiences in Saudi Arabia. In 2023, Pam published *Life is Breath; Everything Else is a Story: My Story, Your Story, Our Story, The Story*, available at Schuler Books & Music located in Grand Rapids.

While Pam and Andy belong to several community organizations and enjoy staying engaged locally, they love traveling near and far, including visiting their four married children and 13 grandchildren, now young adults themselves, all growing up and doing what they love and loving what they do—some coast to coast across the country, some here in Michigan.

Pamela Harman Daugavietis

Printed in the United States
by Baker & Taylor Publisher Services